Cows, Cats, and Kids

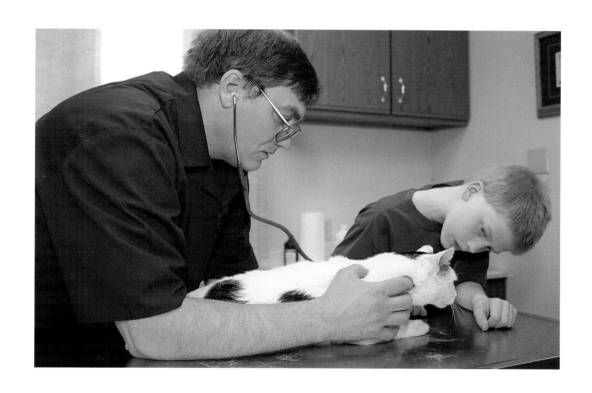

Cows, Cats, and Kids

A Veterinarian's Family at Work

For Peg,
who knows about
the farm
(and loves the open spaces!)

All best,

Jean LS Patrick

by Jean L. S. Patrick

Photographs by Alvis Upitis

BOYDS MILLS PRESS

Text copyright © 2003 by Jean L. S. Patrick

Photographs copyright © 2003 by Alvis Upitis

Boyds Mills Press, Inc.
A Highlights Company
815 Church Street
Honesdale, Pennsylvania 18431

Printed in China

Visit our Web site at www.boydsmillspress.com

Publisher Cataloging-in-Publication Data

Patrick, Jean L. S.
Cows, cats, and kids : a veterinarian's family at work /
by Jean L. S. Patrick ; photographs by Alvis Upitis. — 1st ed.
[48] p. : col. photos. ;   cm.
Includes index.
Summary: A look at the family life of a veterinarian
at home and in the field.
ISBN 1-56397-111-9
1. Veterinarians—Juvenile literature. I. Upitis, Alvis. II. Title.
636.089 21   2003
2002109582

First edition, 2003

Book design by Amy Drinker, Aster Designs

The text of this book is set in 13.5 Janson Text.

10 9 8 7 6 5 4 3 2 1

For Mike's folks, Richard and Delrena Patrick
—J. L. S. P.

For my sister, Zaiga, with love
—A. U.

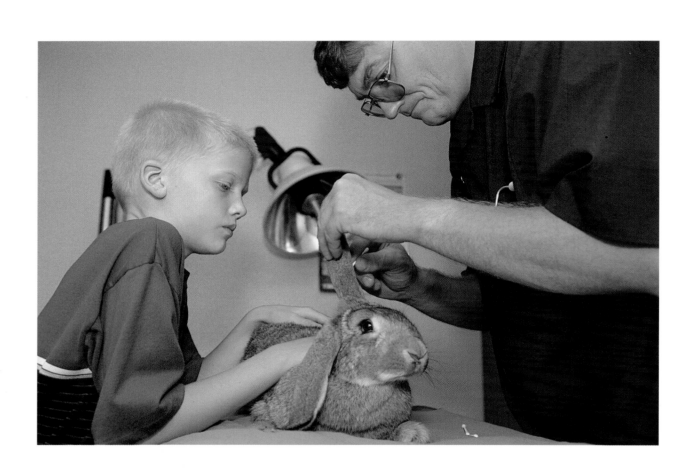

Author's Note

When I was ten years old, my family moved from Chicago to a small town in southern Illinois. Late one afternoon, we took my Border collie to the veterinary clinic for her vaccinations. The clinic was out in the country. The sun was low.

When we arrived, the veterinarian walked out from beside the clinic. He wore jeans and work boots. His daughter, who was about my age, walked next to him.

I was in awe. This girl's dad was a vet. She was with animals all of the time. What did she do each day? Did she help her dad? Did she get to work with farm animals, too?

Little did I know that I'd marry a veterinarian. And little did I know that I'd have three children who would help their father each day, much like the girl I remember.

In this book, you'll learn about the work of my husband, Dr. Mike Patrick, who is a mixed-animal veterinarian in South Dakota. You'll see his work through the eyes of our children—Shea, Kendall, and Catherine.

Shea

Late one spring afternoon, Shea raced into the clinic. "Dad! Tiny's here!"

"She's growing," said Dad. Tiny was a four-month-old Chihuahua and terrier mix. She wasn't much bigger than a tennis ball, but after greeting everyone, she proudly led her owner into the exam room.

Shea liked Tiny. Last week when Tiny had been sick, Dad brought her home so that he could treat her during the night. Dad sat in the easy chair, cuddled Tiny on his chest, and fed her tiny drops of medicine.

Ten-year-old Shea was glad that Tiny was feeling better. But he wondered when Dad would be done with the exam. He wished Dad would play ball with him in the parking lot. Football. Baseball. Any kind of ball.

Shea and Mom welcome Tiny and her owner to the clinic.

8

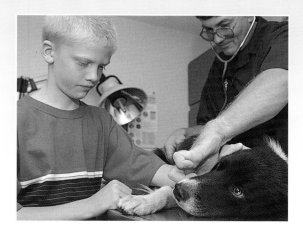

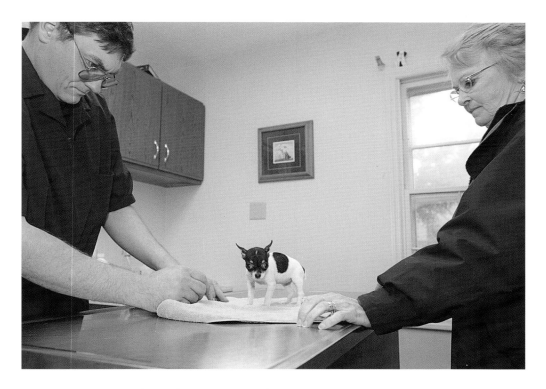

Dad observes Tiny's legs. The previous week, Tiny suffered from hypoglycemia, or low blood sugar, and was unable to stand.

Shea waited in the office. There wasn't much to do. His sister, Catherine, was hogging the computer. His younger brother, Kendall, kneeled on the floor. He was trying to fix the handle on the desk drawer with a screwdriver.

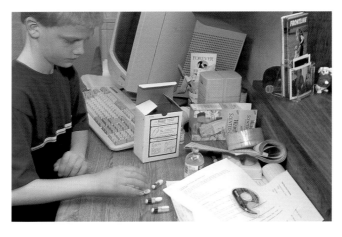

Shea was bored. Really bored. But he didn't dare say it out loud. If he did, Mom would tell him to clean the cages in the kennel room. And then she'd give him a lecture about how fortunate he was that Dad included him in his work.

If only Dad were a professional football player. Shea would love to be included in that kind of work.

But that would never happen. Dad was too busy being a mixed-animal veterinarian. Sometimes he took care of cats, dogs, birds, and hamsters. But most of the time, he was busy with cattle, horses, and other large animals.

Above, Shea counts the large boluses, or pills, that Dad will give to calves with diarrhea. Below, Mom and Shea help in the clinic in many ways.

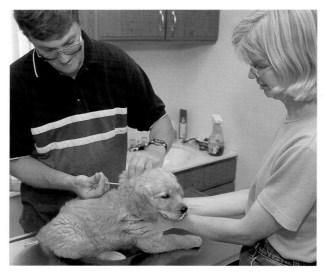

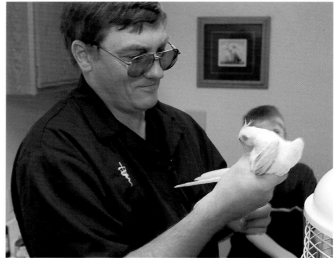

The telephone rang. Mom hurried to the desk.

"Hello, Animal Clinic." Mom's voice became serious. "How long has she been pushing?"

Shea knew the meaning of that question. It was an emergency.

After Tiny and her owner left the clinic, Mom spoke quickly to Dad. "Dave Newsback has a cow that's having problems calving. I told him you'd be right over."

Dad and Mom check the appointments listed in the daybook. A calving emergency can quickly change the afternoon's schedule.

Dad dashed into the back room, stripped off his clinic jacket, and pulled on his old green coveralls. He rummaged through his supplies, stuffing his deep pockets with medicine bottles, syringes, and chains.

Shea knew to stay out of the way.

"Just reschedule the rest of the day's appointments," said Dad. He gave Mom a kiss. "I won't be back until late."

Shea thought fast. If he stayed with Mom, he'd have to clean cages. If he went with Dad, he might get to see a newborn calf. It wasn't a tough decision.

"Can I go?" he asked.

"Get in the truck," said Dad.

Shea raced out the door.

While Dad's pickup truck roared down dirt roads, Shea stared out of the window. This was his favorite part about farm calls. He saw pheasant flying up from the ditches, deer feeding near a row of trees, and calves nestling in the grass along the fence lines.

"Will the calf be alive?" asked Shea.

"We'll see."

Shea felt the truck surge ahead when Dad shifted into fifth gear.

Forty miles later, Dad drove through the Newsbacks' farmyard. A huge Angus cow was standing in a cattle chute in the pen beside the barn. A yellow hoof poked through the opening under her tail.

Dave Newsback jammed his hands deep into his pockets and walked over to Dad's side of the truck. Dad rolled down his window.

Using the Coggins Test

In order to check a horse for EIA (Equine Infectious Anemia), Dad must draw blood for a Coggins test. A horse must test negative for this disease before it is allowed to travel across state lines. After Dad catches and halters the horse, he lets Shea hold the lead rope.

"How's she doing?" Dad asked.

"Still pushing," said Dave. The cow bellowed and tossed her head.

"Can I get out?" Shea whispered. Often he had to stay in the truck, especially if Dad had to rope the cow first. But this cow was already restrained in the chute.

"OK." Dad opened his door. "But stay back."

Dad stepped out of the truck, pulled off his jacket, and covered his arms with long plastic OB sleeves.

"Easy, girl." With his left hand, Dad patted the cow's bony hip, then grabbed her tail. Next, he gently guided his right hand into her birth canal.

Dad concentrated. Shea knew his father was trying to feel the position of the calf. Was a front hoof sticking out? Or was it a rear foot? Was he feeling one calf or two? Shea held his breath.

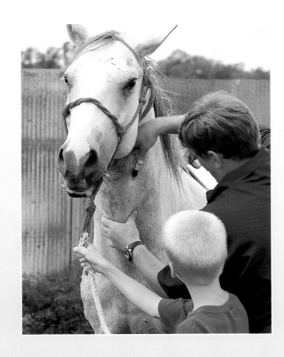

Meanwhile, Dave was silent. His calloused hands gripped the metal railing of the cattle chute.

"It's a front hoof!" said Dad. "The calf's alive!"

Shea relaxed.

But the cow sidestepped, jerking Dad sharply to the left. Wincing, he pulled out his arm and dropped the tail.

"No sense getting hurt, Doc," said Dave.

"We're in good shape." Dad wiped his forehead on his shoulder. "The other front hoof is just a little ways down."

Dad caught the cow's tail and entered the birth canal again. Slowly, he pulled out another yellow hoof. "We're set!"

Shea stepped back as Dad looped a calving chain around each hoof.

"Grab a handle!"

Shea hesitated. Was Dad talking to Dave?

"Let's go, Shea!" said Dad. "Pull!"

Shea grabbed the handle of one of the calving chains while Dad clenched the other. With both hands, Shea pulled.

"Harder!" yelled Dad. "Pull harder!"

Shea pulled harder. Now was his chance to impress Dad. Now he could show Dad how strong he was. But the yellow hooves didn't budge.

Calving chains allow Dad and Shea to "pull" the calf. Without chains, they cannot grip the calf's wet, slippery hooves and help with the delivery.

"Keep pulling!" He heard Dad straining beside him. "Don't give up!"

Shea's fingers cramped. His forearms trembled. How much longer could he pull?

Slowly, the hooves slid forward, followed by legs. The nose came next, black and wet. The rest of the calf's head followed, covered with clear slime.

"Be ready to catch him, Dave," Dad yelled. "Here he comes!"

Dave stretched out his arms, cradled the calf, and eased him to the ground. But the calf didn't move.

What was the matter? Why wasn't he breathing?

"Try rubbing his ribs," Dad suggested to Shea. But that didn't help.

Dad dug his fingers into the calf's mouth and nose, clearing out the amniotic fluid.

"We'll let gravity drain the rest," said Dad to Dave.

Shea rubs the calf's rib cage, hoping to stimulate breathing.

"When I say three, lift."

Dad and Dave each gripped a back leg.

"One . . . two . . . three . . . LIFT!"

They draped the calf over the gate. The calf's motionless head pointed toward the ground.

"Shea!" commanded Dad. "Get some straw!"

Shea grabbed a handful.

"Go ahead," urged Dad. "Fast!"

Clutching the straw, Shea tickled one nostril. Nothing happened. He jabbed the other. But the calf still wouldn't breathe. Now what should he do?

Gravity helps to drain the amniotic fluid from the calf's lungs.

Frantically, Shea pushed the straw deep into both of the calf's nostrils.

Sniff.

The calf's nose twitched.

Sniff. Sniff-sniff.

16

The calf sneezed.

Shea wiped his arm and laughed. Finally, the calf was breathing.

Fifteen minutes later, the calf was wiggling and shaking his head, nearly nosediving into the pen. Dad and Dave wrestled him to the ground. The calf stuck out his tongue and bellowed.

Shea grinned.

When Dad released the mama cow, she circled twice around the pen. When she saw her new baby, she stopped. She sniffed him and licked him, massaging his rib cage with her long, rough tongue.

Shea tickles the calf's nose to help him start breathing.

17

The first milk a calf drinks from its mother is called colostrum. This milk is rich with antibodies to protect the calf from disease.

Dad turned to leave. "Be sure the calf starts nursing within six hours."

"Thanks, Doc," said Dave, waving. "And thank your boy, too. You've got some good help there."

Shea smiled. Maybe it was a good thing that he wasn't the son of a professional football player. Without calving calls, he might get bored.

Kendall

Early the next morning, Kendall lay in bed, listening to Dad talk on the telephone. If he listened carefully, he might be able to figure out Dad's plans.

"If it's just thirty head, we can get them done before the trucks come," Dad said. "Just vaccinate, pour, and tag?"

Eight-year-old Kendall knew exactly what Dad was talking about. Calf work! Thirty calves needed vaccinations, lice protection, and fly tags before they were moved to their summer pasture. And since the stock trucks were coming this morning, the calves needed to be worked right away.

In the spring, it seemed as if Dad spent most of his time with beef cattle. He needed to help ranchers keep their herds healthy.

Kendall grabbed a workshirt and tiptoed past Shea, who was still sleeping underneath his Minnesota Vikings blanket. Working calves wasn't nearly as exciting as pulling a calf, but Kendall didn't care. He just wanted to be with Dad.

"Can I go?" whispered Kendall.

Dad nodded. "Get in the truck."

Together, they slammed their doors, buckled their seat belts, and yawned. Kendall's yawn was loud. But Dad's was ten times louder. Kendall knew that Dad didn't get much sleep. Late last night, he had to go back to the clinic to take care of a kitten that had been caught in a reclining chair.

When they reached the pasture, Dad pulled down the tailgate of the truck. A group of thirty calves were in the catch

Kendall helps Dad take the vaccines and medicines out of the truck. Everything is carefully labeled.

21

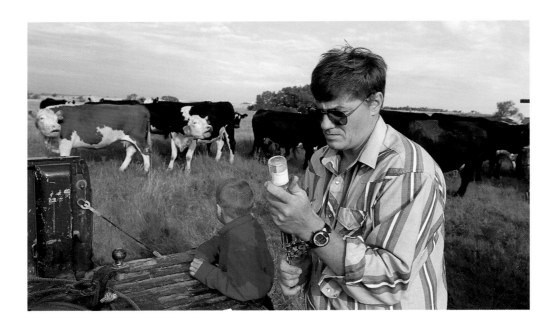

pen, bawling for their mamas. Thirty cows waited at the end of the chute, bellowing for their babies.

Kendall plugged his ears and watched Dad prepare his tools. First, Dad filled his pistol-grip syringe with vaccine. Next, he set out a long-handled ladle, a new box of fly tags, and a pair of tagging pliers.

Kendall sighed. He loved tools, especially pliers. He liked to squeeze the handles and watch the tips come together.

But Dad handed him a long metal bar. "Ready?"

"*Hyaw!*" Kendall and the rancher yelled, urging the calves down the alleyway. The calves pushed forward, brushing against the panels and kicking up dirt. The mama cows waited and bellowed.

Clunk-clunk. Clunk-clunk. The first calf stepped into the

cattle chute. Kendall shoved his bar behind the calf so he couldn't back up. Meanwhile, Dad pulled the headgate shut, securing the calf's neck.

Kendall watched. With the pistol-grip syringe, Dad vaccinated the calf against a disease called blackleg. He used the ladle to pour lice insecticide down the mid-line of the calf's back. Finally, he grabbed the pliers and attached a fly tag to the calf's ear.

Kendall watches as the calves are pushed up the alleyway toward the yellow cattle chute.

When Dad released the headgate, the calf ran to his mama, his fly tag flopping like an earring. Kendall laughed. The calf probably didn't know that his new earring contained insecticide to keep away hornflies and faceflies.

Kendall pulled out his bar and let another

calf enter the chute. Dad vaccinated, poured, and tagged. Kendall loved the work. Maybe he could do this next week, too. After all, Dad often had to work more than a hundred calves at a time. Maybe Dad would even pay him.

One by one, the calves moved through the chute, then trotted back to their mothers. All became quiet.

"They look good," said Dad. He and the rancher leaned against the truck, admiring the small herd.

Kendall knew that these calves were important. When the rancher sold them in the fall, they would be worth a lot of money. But Kendall's stomach was rumbling. He was hungry for breakfast.

Kendall and Dad rushed back to town, picked up a box of doughnuts at the drive-through, and headed to the clinic. Mom was waiting. So were Shea and Catherine. So were a

A calf is momentarily restrained by the headgate while the veterinarian does his work.

Weimaraner puppy, a white tomcat, and their owners.

"I'll be right with you!" said Dad.

Kendall and Dad ducked into the back room where they washed up and changed into clean clothes. Kendall kicked the dirt-covered jeans into a corner.

Kendall knew that taking care of small animals was a lot different than working cattle. And it wasn't just because of the dirt and manure. When Dad examined a pet, he was caring for a member of someone's family.

Kendall joined Dad in the exam room. He liked to watch his father give special attention to each animal. Dad was gentle when

Kendall and Catherine watch Dad vaccinate a springer spaniel against parvovirus and distemper.

he treated the Weimaraner
puppy with bleeding gums,
the tomcat that had no
energy to walk, and a pet
goat that lay injured in the
back of a pickup truck.

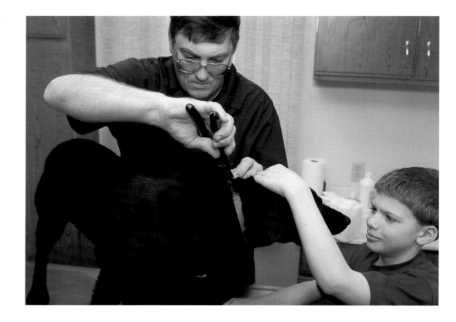

Kendall also liked the
little tools Dad used.
When a cat needed
antibiotics, Dad used a
small syringe. When a rab-
bit doe's ears needed cleaning, he used a long cotton swab. And
when he felt the sharp toenails of a dachsund, he reached into
the drawer for his nail trimmers.

*The rabies tag
that Dad is
attaching shows
proof of the dog's
vaccination.*

More dogs and cats arrived. They needed vaccinations
against rabies and other diseases.

Dad held a hunting dog on the table. "Give me a hand,
Kendall!"

Kendall read Dad's mind. He ran to the office to get a rabies
tag, an S-hook, and a pair of pliers. Kendall watched as Dad
squeezed the pliers, attaching the tag to the dog's collar.

Kendall chuckled. Dad always seemed to need a good pair
of pliers.

This made Kendall think. There were some ways that farm
animals and pets were a lot alike. They all needed vaccines and

tools to keep them healthy.

Kendall wasn't the only one who liked being with Dad. Cats liked him because he was calm. Dogs liked him because he talked to them and scratched their backs.

Dad's clients liked him, too. One woman brought him farm-fresh eggs. Another woman gave him old blankets for the kennels.

Sometimes, Dad would stand in the parking lot, listening to ranchers ask complicated questions about calf medicine. Other times, he would sit in the clinic lobby, listening to people talk

What Happens During a Checkup?

When a cat arrives for a checkup, Dad examines him from nose to tail. Dad also tries to prevent future problems. He checks the ears for mites, inspects the mouth for sores and dental problems, and applies medicine to prevent fleas and ticks.

about their grandchildren, crops, and the weather.

Kendall wasn't very good at sitting and listening. But he was getting better at being respectful to clients. For him, that meant no yelling, no burping, and no bouncing tennis balls inside the clinic.

Kendall tried hard to be polite when his piano teacher brought Hobbs, her music-loving cat, for his exam. After his teacher paid the bill, Kendall held open the door.

"Thank you," said Mrs. Paris.

Kendall grinned. "You're welcome."

Later that morning, Dad sat at the computer. He took a bite of doughnut and pulled open his money drawer.

"How about getting these checks ready for the bank?" Dad asked.

Kendall found the ink pad and the check stamp in the

Left, Dad examines a baby goat with a broken leg. He will stabilize the leg before carrying the goat into the clinic.

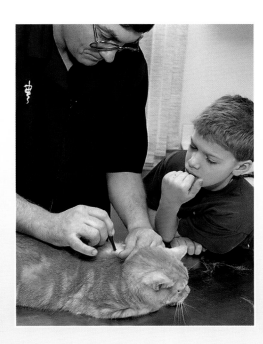

The computer is an important tool for the veterinarian. It holds and retrieves information about billing, treatments, and vaccinations.

drawer. More tools! Carefully, he stamped the name of the clinic on the back of each check.

Kendall looked at the thick stack of checks. It seemed as if Dad earned a lot of money, but Kendall knew that Dad had plenty of bills to pay, too. Dad had to pay for medicines, vaccines, and gas for his truck. He had to pay for the electricity, the water, the telephone, and the clinic building. He even had to pay for doughnuts and pliers.

At least he doesn't have to pay me, thought Kendall.

After he finished stamping checks, it was finally time to play. Kendall ate the rest of Dad's doughnut, found a tennis ball under the desk, and ran outside with Shea.

Catherine

At that moment, Catherine was not particularly pleased to be part of the family. She'd much rather be at home, getting her horse ready for 4-H or playing with the barn kittens.

Instead, she slouched on a chair in the clinic lobby.

Her friends always told her how lucky she was that her dad was a veterinarian. Little did they know what really went on during a typical day.

The boys were outside throwing tennis balls against the wall of the clinic, giving her a major headache. Dad was patting his chest with a piece of mailing tape, trying to remove Hobbs's cat hair from his shirt.

He also was asking Mom to go the bank, the post office, and to the store to get paper towels. "And please take the boys," he said.

Life was looking up.

"Catherine?" Dad tossed the hair-covered tape into the trash. "I need your help with a cat spay."

Twelve-year-old Catherine loved surgeries. She had seen hundreds of them. Spays. Neuters. Tumor removals. In fact, she was sure she could perform surgery—if only Dad would talk her through it. Of course, Dad always said no.

Catherine placed Macey on the scale.

"Five-point-nine pounds," she said.

Dad double-checked the cat's weight, then calculated the correct amount of anesthetic. Even though Dad spent his days with animals, he was always using math.

Catherine helped Dad shave the underside of the cat and then wipe the skin with surgical cleanser. She watched as he carefully cut the skin, the tissue, and the muscle wall.

"Hold this, please," said Dad.

Catherine weighs a cat before surgery. The weight determines the amount of anesthetic that Dad will use.

Catherine held a clamp while Dad removed the cat's uterus and ovaries. Macey would no longer be able to have kittens.

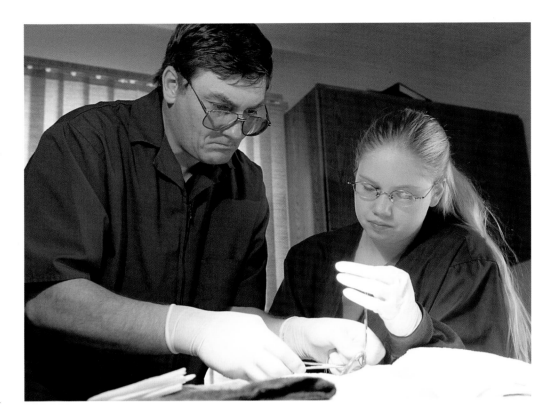

With a curved needle, Dad closed the incision. Five blue knots now decorated Macey's shaved belly.

Catherine provides Dad with a "third hand." She holds a clamp while Dad ties off a blood vessel.

The door to the clinic squeaked open.

"Anybody home?"

Catherine washed her hands and dashed to the lobby. A woman placed a cardboard box on the floor. It jiggled with Labrador retriever puppies.

"They're four days old," said the woman, rather proudly. "They're here to get their dewclaws removed."

Dad came out of the surgery room, drying his hands on a paper towel. He peered into the box. "Now that's a pile of puppies! We'll have them done in an hour."

Catherine smiled. She liked the way Dad included her with his words. She pulled on latex gloves and cradled the first pup on his back. His eyes were wrinkled shut.

Gently, Dad felt for the dewclaw, the tiny "thumb" that protruded from the pup's leg. "Hold him still," Dad commanded.

Catherine used to wonder if it would be kinder to leave the dewclaws on.

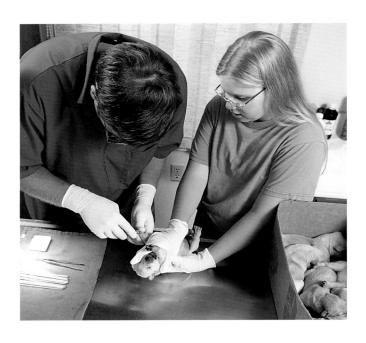

Dad had explained. Labradors were hunting dogs. If their dewclaws were not removed, they'd get hooked on the tall grass. A torn nail would cause much more pain than preventive surgery.

When Puppies Have Worms . . .

Worms aren't fun! If hookworms or roundworms are living in a puppy's digestive tract, they can cause decreased energy and poor growth. As a result, Dad recommends that all puppies be dewormed. Under Dad's supervision, Catherine gives a liquid deworming medication to a springer spaniel puppy.

Left, *Catherine gently holds the puppy while Dad removes a dewclaw.*
Right, *A pile of yellow Labrador puppies snuggle together after surgery.*

Catherine set the last puppy in the box. Together, they whined and grumbled. Soon they slept, dreaming of lunch with their mother.

The clinic door squeaked open again. Shea and Kendall

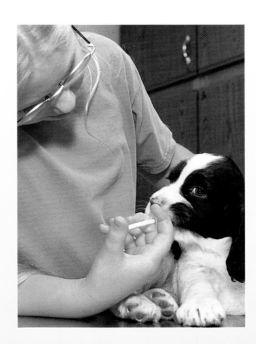

charged to the computer. Mom collapsed on Dad's desk chair with a grocery sack of bananas, bread, sliced turkey, and paper towels.

After Catherine made the sandwiches on the edge of Dad's desk, Mom prayed aloud. Dad swallowed his sandwich in three gulps and looked at the daybook. "I have to go to the Andersons' farm to look at a new shipment of pigs," said Dad. "Which boy is coming with me?"

Catherine threw her banana peel into the trash and headed to the kennel room to clean cages. She was furious. Dad always took one of the boys on farm calls. Always!

It was all Mom's fault. She said it was impossible to run the clinic and take care of two wild boys at the same time.

Mom did have a point. But it wasn't fair. Catherine loved being with Dad in the truck, driving down dirt roads, talking about horses and dogs and donkeys. Face it. Being with Dad was more fun than listening to Mom answer the phone.

Catherine walked back into the office. She tried to be calm. "Could I go with Dad this time?" For a moment,

Above, Catherine disinfects cages in the kennel room. Right, Dad checks the identification number that is tattooed on a piglet's ear. Lower right, Long plastic sleeves protect Dad's arms from disease as he examines a dead calf.

the boys were quiet.

"We'll give it a try," Mom said. "Get in the truck."

After Dad inspected the piglets in the Andersons' nursery barn, he and Catherine drove south down a country road.

"What's next?" asked Catherine.

"I have to post a calf," said Dad.

Catherine sighed. Finally, she was going on calls with Dad, and he had to do a postmortem. In other words, he'd have to examine a dead calf to find out why it died.

She knew she shouldn't complain. After all, Dad's client needed to know why the calf had died. He couldn't afford to lose more calves in the same way.

Dad drove into a bumpy pasture, then parked upwind from the calf. She could hear the flies.

"Want to come watch?"

Catherine shook her head. Posting a calf really wasn't that exciting. In fact, her friends would faint if they knew the

truth about Dad's
veterinary work.

When the cell
phone rings, it's
usually Mom,
directing Dad
to his next
farm call.

Besides posting
calves, Dad lanced
lumps, sutured eyes,
and reached into the
back end of cows.
And those were the
easy calls. On some
days, his coveralls were so covered with blood and manure that
he had to spray them down at the car wash.

Catherine heard Dad's cell phone ring. It was probably Mom,
relaying a message about the next call.

At the Longhofers' farm, Dad kneeled in front of a Suffolk ram.

Catherine watched him part the wool. Confidently, he inserted a needle into the ram's jugular vein. He pulled back the syringe, collecting a sample of the ram's dark blood.

Dad acted more like a detective than a veterinarian as he was gathering clues. Later on, he would send the blood serum to the State Diagnostic Laboratory to be tested for a disease called brucellosis. If the test came back positive, the ram could not be used for breeding.

Catherine used the ram's broad back as a desk. On each test tube, she carefully wrote the owner's name, the date, and the ram's age, breed, and identification number. It was amazing how

Left, *Dad takes a blood sample from the ram.* Right, *As Catherine labels the test tube, her forearms sink into the ram's thick wool.*

a small sample of blood could protect the future of a flock.

Three rams later, Dad and Catherine climbed back into the truck.

"Where next?" said Catherine.

"Annie's," said Dad. "She needs a horse gelded."

Catherine loved to go to Annie's. Huskies and chows barked from the kennels. Quarter horses grazed in the wide pastures.

Annie walked out of the barn, leading a small paint stallion with a bright white mane.

Taking the lead rope, Catherine led the young stallion to a clean grassy area, away from the buildings and fences. Dad talked to him gently, tapping him on the neck several times before injecting the anesthetic.

Left, *Dad follows as Catherine leads the yearling stallion.* Right, *Catherine assists with the surgery. By restraining the horse's head, Catherine prevents the horse from getting up too soon.*

As Dad performed the surgery, Catherine sat near the horse's head. She covered his eyes with a towel. Even though the afternoon was cool, his eyes could dry out or be injured by the sun.

Thirty minutes later, the horse was awake with his head up. When thirty more minutes passed, Dad led him back to the barn.

"Anything else you need?"

"Rabies shots for the horses and dogs," said Annie. "But could you take a look at one of my mares? She's been losing weight."

"It's probably her teeth," said Dad. They followed Annie to the pasture north of the barn. Dad slipped his finger into the side of the mare's mouth.

But Catherine's eyes followed the mare's foal, standing several yards away. In the sunlight, his gray-black coat looked almost red. He was covered with light fuzz, almost like the fluff of a kitten.

Catherine wanted to touch him.

Slowly, she walked toward the foal.

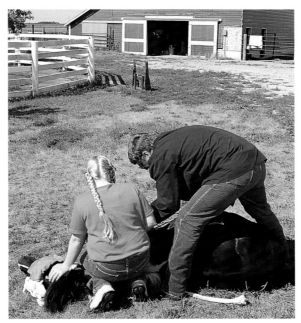

One ear cocked toward his mother. Catherine froze. If she entered his flight zone, he'd run.

But if she kneeled, maybe he'd come to her. Maybe he'd think she was another horse. Or at least a little animal.

The foal walked forward.

One step. Two steps. She could see his long eyelashes. He took another step. She counted five whiskers on his muzzle. She saw the smooth velvet that lined his nostrils.

Just one more step and she'd be able to feel his warm breath. Just one more step and she'd be able to touch him.

The foal stopped. Suddenly, he threw back his head, wheeled around, and galloped back to his mother.

Catherine turned back to her father. Together, they walked through the pasture, then back to the horses near the barn. Catherine watched as Dad vaccinated Annie's horses. She waited while he answered questions about one of Annie's

As Dad moves slowly among the horses, he earns their trust.

45

Dad talks to Annie about a vaccination schedule for her growing chow.

chows. A cat slid around a fence post.

Back in the truck, country music blared from the radio. Catherine buckled her seat belt and half-shut her eyes.

Her friends were right. It was great to be a veterinarian's daughter.

She listened as Dad called Mom. "I'm heading back to the clinic. Anything going on?"

Dad listened and smiled, then snapped his phone shut. "No sick animals," he said. "But the boys have five tennis balls stuck on the roof."

Catherine laughed. "Sounds like an emergency to me!"

Glossary

amniotic fluid The fluid that surrounds the calf as it grows inside of the cow.

anesthetic A drug that is used to stop the sensation of pain.

cattle chute A piece of equipment that restrains cattle during examinations and other procedures.

clamp A tool used to hold tissue or control bleeding during surgery.

gelding A stallion that has been neutered.

headgate The part of the cattle chute that restrains the animal's neck and head.

insecticide A product that kills or repels insects, grubs, or lice.

mixed-animal veterinarian A doctor who takes care of companion animals (dogs, cats, horses) and food animals (cattle, sheep, hogs).

OB (obstetrical) sleeves Long plastic gloves that cover and protect a veterinarian's arms when working inside of a cow or other animal. The sleeves also protect the animal from substances on the veterinarian.

rabies A deadly disease that affects an animal's brain. The disease may easily be transmitted to humans.

syringe A plastic or glass instrument that is used to inject vaccines and medications or to draw blood from an animal.

vaccine A product that helps to prevent an animal from becoming infected with a disease.